70's Trivia

A Throwback to The Golden Days of The 1970s

Morgana Sanchez

Introduction

Dear beloved readers,

In the hustling and bustling world we are living today, things seem to change rapidly in every single second. I'm very glad that you're here to take a look back at the passing golden days of the 1970s again.

This *1970's Trivia Book* is made for the sake of reminding you of the sleeping memories about the art acts in that timeline. We will take you back from the past by providing you with a bunch of trivia questions and also many interesting facts related to the 70's theme.

Are you ready? Here we go!!!

Table of Contents

I. Random Trivia Quiz

1. Which of these singers won a Grammy Award in country category in the '70s?

   A. Olivia Newton-John.

   B. Christine McVie.

   C. Carole King.

   D. Michael Jackson.

2. What's the name of the house band on The Muppet Show?

   A. The Electric Mayhem.

   B. The Can-Doodles.

   C. The Masquerades.

   D. The Carpenters.

3. What disco diva had a hit with "Turn The Beat Around"?

   A. Anita Ward.

   B. Donna Summer.

   C. Vicki Sue Robinson.

   D. Cheryl Lynn.

4. Which of these girls' names shows up in the title of a Van Halen song?

A. Jamie.

B. Barbara.

C. Aubrey.

D. Martha.

5. What group had a hit with "Native New Yorker" in 1977?

A. Shalamar.

B. Odyssey.

C. The Spinners.

D. The Doobie Brothers.

6. Which of these bands had a member named Buck Dharma?

A. Pink Floyd.

B. Deep Purple.

C. Poco.

D. Blue Öyster Cult.

7. What band did mention the mythical land of Valhal
   in one of their songs?

   A. Led Zeppelin.

   B. Rush.

   C. Earth, Wind & Fire.

   D. Black Sabbath.

8. What band was named Best New Artist of 1978 b
   both Rolling Stone and Creem magazines?

   A. Boston.

   B. The Cars.

   C. Aerosmith.

   D. Genesis.

9. Which of these lead singers was also an accomplishe
   drummer?

   A. Ann Wilson of Heart.

   B. Cynthia Ross of B-Girls.

   C. Debbie Harry of Blondie.

   D. Karen Carpenter of the Carpenters.

10. Which of these singers had a #1 UK hit in the '70s as a solo artist?

    A. Dolly Parton.

    B. Art Garfunkel.

    C. John Oates.

    D. Dash Crofts.

11. Who wrote "Mama Told Me (Not to Come)" the 1970 US No.1 hit for Three Dog Night?

    A. Tom Jones.

    B. Randy Newman.

    C. Andy Luck.

    D. Randy Newman.

12. On which Stevie Wonder album would you find his 1976 US No.1 hit "I Wish"?

    A. Fulfillingness' First Finale.

    B. Talking Book.

    C. Songs in the Key of Life.

    D. Innervisions.

13. Which track from the Paul McCartney and Linc McCartney album Ram was a US No.1 in 1970?

    A. "The Back Seat of My Car".

    B. "Too Many People".

    C. "Dear Boy".

    D. "Uncle Albert/Admiral Halsey".

14. Who scored the US No.1 hit "The Loco-Motion" 1974?

    A. Bachman-Turner Overdrive.

    B. Grand Funk.

    C. Blue Swede.

    D. Marvin Gaye.

15. Which Eagles song gave the band their first US No hit single of the 70's?

    A. "Lyin' Eyes".

    B. "One of These Nights".

    C. "Tequila Sunrise".

    D. "Best of My Love".

16. Which Motown star did Hank Cosby co-write "The Tears of a Clown" - the 1970 No.1 hit for Smokey Robinson & the Miracles?

A. Michael Jackson.

B. Stevie Wonder.

C. Marvin Gaye.

D. Levi Stubbs.

17. From which film was "Wand'rin' Star" featured which gave Lee Marvin a UK No.1 hit in 1970?

A. Paint Your Wagon.

B. Huckleberry Finn.

C. Cabaret.

D. None of the above.

18. Who scored the US No.1 album Abraxas in 1970?

A. Blood, Sweat & Tears.

B. The Jackson 5.

C. Santana.

D. Sly & the Family Stone.

19. Who wrote the song "Woodstock" which gave Matthews' Southern Comfort a UK No.1 in 1970?

    A. Neil Young.

    B. Joni Mitchell.

    C. Stevie Wonder.

    D. Crosby, Stills & Nash.

20. Who scored the US 1976 No.1 hit "Let Your Love Flow"?

    A. The Carpenters.

    B. Glen Campbell.

    C. James Taylor.

    D. The Bellamy Brothers.

21. Which group first recorded and wrote "Without You" which became a US & UK No.1 hit for Harry Nilsson?

    A. The Osmonds.

    B. The Bee Gees.

    C. 10cc.

    D. Badfinger.

22. Who had the UK No.1 hit in 1977 with "Yes Sir, I Can Boogie"?

A. Chic.

B. Baccara.

C. Bread.

D. The Floaters.

23. David Soul scored No.1 hits in the 70's. Who did he play in the TV Cop show Starsky & Hutch?

A. Huggy Bear.

B. Kenneth "Hutch" Hutchinson.

C. David Michael Starsky.

D. The Silver Fox.

24. For how many weeks did Simon & Garfunkel's Bridge over Troubled Water stay on the US album chart?

A. 65.

B. 75.

C. 85.

D. 95.

25. On which Led Zeppelin 70's No.1 album would you find the track "Since I've Been Loving You"?

A. Led Zeppelin II.

B. Led Zeppelin III.

C. Led Zeppelin IV.

D. None of the above.

26. Who scored the 1979 US No.1 album Breakfast America?

A. Bay City Rollers.

B. Blues Brothers.

C. Doobie Brothers.

D. Supertramp.

27. Who scored the 1974 US No.1 album "Can't Get Enough"?

A. Bad Company.

B. Gordon Lightfoot.

C. Barry White.

D. Seals & Crofts.

28. Which Beatles song gave them their 20th and last US No.1 in 1970?

    A. "Let it Be".

    B. "Something".

    C. "The Long and Winding Road".

    D. "Chains".

29. Audiences were hopelessly devoted to this musical comedy in the summer of 1978. Can you name it?

    A. "Grease".

    B. "Fiddler on the Roof".

    C. "Bugsy Malone".

    D. "The Wiz".

30. Can you name the mob movie that made audiences an offer they couldn't refuse in 1972?

    A. "Mean Streets".

    B. "The Godfather".

    C. "Get Carter".

    D. "The Mechanic".

31. The Bee Gees cemented their reputation as the king of disco with the soundtrack to this 1977 film. Can you name this movie?

    A. "Sgt Pepper's Lonely Hearts Club Band".

    B. "Saturday Night Fever".

    C. "Can't Stop the Music".

    D. "Roller Boogie".

32. Can you name this 1973 horror film that pitted young priest against a demon in a battle for a young girl's soul?

    A. "The Omen".

    B. "Rosemary's Baby".

    C. "Beyond the Door".

    D. "The Exorcist".

33. Can you name this '70s action comedy in which Burt Reynolds and Jerry Reed have a long way to go and a short time to get there?

    A. "Smokey and the Bandit".

    B. "Gator".

    C. "Hot Stuff".

    D. "Cannonball Run".

34. John Belushi is no fan of folk music in this 1978 college comedy from John Landis. Can you name it?

    A. "Used Cars".

    B. "Animal House".

    C. "The Kentucky Fried Movie".

    D. "Schlock".

35. Which of these singers gave us "Hot Stuff" in 1979?

    A. Blondie.

    B. Donna Summer.

    C. Olivia Newton-John.

    D. Linda Ronstadt.

36. Sylvester Stallone wrote and starred in this 197 Academy Award-winning drama. Can you name it?

A. "No Place to Hide".

B. "The Lords of Flatbush".

C. "Rocky".

D. "F.I.S.T".

37. Can you name the 1978 film that made audienc believe a man could fly?

A. "Superman, The Movie".

B. "Doc Savage".

C. "Supersonic Man".

D. "Infra-Man".

38. Richard Dreyfuss knows the truth is out there in th 1977 sci-fi hit. Can you name this film?

A. "Silent Running".

B. "Soylent Green".

C. "The Andromeda Strain".

D. "Close Encounters of the Third Kind".

39. Can you name the science-fiction epic that brought a beloved '60s TV series to the silver screen in 1979?

A. "Lost in Space".

B. "A Boy and His Dog".

C. "Twilight Zone: The Movie".

D. "Star Trek: The Motion Picture".

40. Richard Roundtree takes on the mob in this blaxploitation hit from 1971. Can you name this film?

A. "Super Fly".

B. "Coffy".

C. "Three the Hard Way".

D. "Shaft".

41. Can you name the 1970 wartime comedy film that spawned a successful, long-running TV show?

A. "No Time for Segments".

B. "1941".

C. "Kelly's Heroes".

D. "M*A*S*H".

42. Which of these groups was formed by the Gib brothers: Barry, Maurice and Robin?

A. The Bee Gees.

B. The Jackson 5.

C. The Village People.

D. Captain & Tennille.

43. Can you spot the singer whose 1970s hits includ "Signed, Sealed, Delivered I'm Yours?"

A. Kenny Rogers.

B. Rod Stewart.

C. Stevie Wonder.

D. Al Green.

44. Which Beatles co-founder had the world singir "Imagine" in 1971?

A. Marvin Gaye.

B. The Commodores.

C. James Brown.

D. John Lennon.

45. Who released "Candle in the Wind" in both 1974 and 1997?

    A. The Carpenters.

    B. Foreigner.

    C. Elton John.

    D. Tom Petty and The Heartbreakers.

46. Which "Piano Man" promised to love you "Just the Way You Are" in 1977?

    A. David Bowie.

    B. The Temptations.

    C. Barry Manilow.

    D. Billy Joel.

47. Which English rock group offered us "Brown Sugar" in 1971?

    A. Lynyrd Skynyrd.

    B. The Rolling Stones.

    C. The Bee Gees.

    D. Aerosmith.

48. Which costumed group promoted the "Y.M.C.A" ar got "In the Navy?"

A. The Village People.

B. Queen.

C. The Police.

D. Al Green.

49. Who sang about the "Rich Girl" and told us "She Gone" in the 1970s?

A. Rod Stewart.

B. Hall & Oates.

C. Al Green.

D. John Lennon.

50. Who took fans to the "Copacabana (At the Copa)" 1978?

A. The Village People

B. Kenny Rogers.

C. Alice Cooper.

D. Barry Manilow.

51. Who proclaimed "We Are the Champions" while promising "We Will Rock You?"

    A. The Temptations.

    B. Queen.

    C. Captain & Tennille.

    D. Elton John.

52. Which well-dressed group released "Three Times a Lady" in 1978?

    A. The Commodores.

    B. Lynyrd Skynyrd.

    C. The Police.

    D. The Who.

53. Who told us it "Feels Like the First Time" on their 1977 debut single?

    A. Alice Cooper.

    B. Aerosmith.

    C. Foreigner.

    D. Teddy Pendergrass.

54. Which country crooner's list of 1970s hits include "Lucille"?

    A. John Lennon.

    B. Kenny Rogers.

    C. Marvin Gaye.

    D. Chicago.

55. Which glam rock artist was also known by his alter ego Ziggy Stardust?

    A. The Carpenters.

    B. Billy Joel.

    C. David Bowie.

    D. Barry Manilow.

56. Which group of brothers made music as easy as "ABC" in 1970?

    A. Elton John.

    B. James Brown.

    C. The Who.

    D. The Jackson 5.

57. Which British rock artist asked "Do Ya Think I'm Sexy?" in 1978?

    A. The Rolling Stones.

    B. Lynyrd Skynyrd.

    C. Rod Stewart.

    D. Stevie Wonder.

58. Who invited his listeners to "Turn Off the Lights" in 1979?

    A. Teddy Pendergrass.

    B. The Temptations.

    C. ABBA.

    D. John Lennon.

59. Which group of Bad Boys from Boston told us to "Walk This Way" in 1975?

    A. Hall & Oates.

    B. Kenny Rogers.

    C. The Bee Gees.

    D. Aerosmith.

60. Which Swedish quartet sang about the "Dancir Queen" in 1976?

    A. ABBA.

    B. Linda Ronstadt.

    C. The Jackson 5.

    D. Barry Manilow.

61. Which rock band led by Debbie Harry sang about "Heart of Glass" in 1979?

    A. Barbra Streisand.

    B. Diana Ross.

    C. Olivia Newton-John.

    D. Blondie.

62. Which rock band based its name on a high school P. teacher?

    A. The Commodores.

    B. Lynyrd Skynyrd.

    C. The Village People.

    D. Kenny Rogers.

63. Which brother and sister duo declared "We've Only Just Begun" in 1970?

    A. Foreigner.

    B. Diana Ross.

    C. Tom Petty and The Heartbreakers.

    D. The Carpenters.

64. Who urged "Let's Get It On" in 1973?

    A. The Village People.

    B. Marvin Gaye.

    C. The Who.

    D. The Temptations.

65. Who sang about "The Way We Were" in 1973?

    A. Barbra Streisand.

    B. Linda Ronstadt.

    C. Olivia Newton-John.

    D. Donna Summer.

66. Which shock rocker claimed to be "No More Mr. Nice Guy" in 1973?

    A. Queen.

    B. Hall & Oates.

    C. Alice Cooper.

    D. Billy Joel.

67. Who declared "Just My Imagination (Running Away with Me)" in 1971?

    A. Stevie Wonder.

    B. David Bowie.

    C. The Temptations.

    D. The Rolling Stones.

68. Which "Super Bad" singer was called the "Godfather of Soul"?

    A. The Commodores.

    B. James Brown.

    C. Elton John.

    D. Teddy Pendergrass.

69. Which group sang about an "American Girl" in 1977?

    A. Tom Petty and The Heartbreakers.

    B. The Jackson 5.

    C. The Police.

    D. The Carpenters.

70. Which "Ain't No Mountain High Enough" singer started out with the Supremes?

    A. Stevie Wonder.

    B. Foreigner.

    C. Diana Ross.

    D. Tom Petty and The Heartbreakers.

I. Music Facts

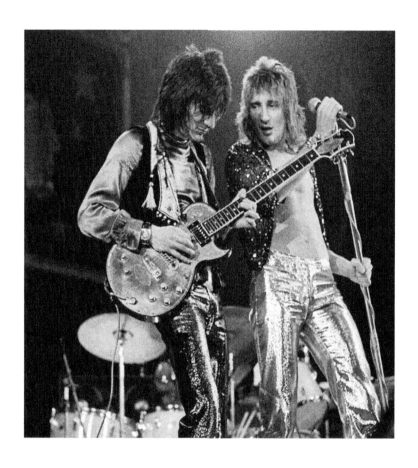

1. Polyester became extremely popular in the '70
   because it was such an inexpensive and durable fib
   that was being advertised as "a miracle fiber that ca
   be worn for 68 days straight without ironing, and st
   look presentable".

2. Cheap Trick's name for their band was inspired by their attendance at a Slade concert where Tom Petersson commented that the band used "every cheap trick in the book" as part of their act.

3. In 1977, "Blinded By The Light," "Dancing Queen," "Hotel California," and "You Light Up My Life" all appeared at #1 on the Billboard Hot 100 Chart.

4. Did you know Randy Bachman was a part of the bands Triumph, BTO, and The Guess Who?

5. The term "Yacht Rock" was coined by JD Ryznar, a Los Angeles based writer, actor, and director after he noticed several similarities between Steely Dan and groups like the Doobie Brothers and Toto. These similarities include that a lot of the music of the era featured albums with guys on boats on the cover and songs about sailing and the fact that their music sounded really good on boats since it was good for relaxing, sitting back, and drinking.

6. Elton John charted a Top 40 single every year from 1970 to 1997.

7. The Eagles started out as a backup band for Linda Ronstadt.

8. Led Zeppelin came up with the title "Black Dog" after a large black Labrador walked into the studio while recording.

9. The letters in the name ABBA stand for the ban
member's first names: Agnetha, Benny, Bjorn, an
Anni-Frid.

10. Bob Dylan's "Like a Rolling Stone" was the first t
break the 3-minute limit on FM radio.

11. Queen is proof that not all rock bands are schoo
dropouts. All the members of Queen, except for lea
singer Freddie Mercury, have post-graduate degrees.

12. Funk, Soul, Hard Rock, Soft Rock, and Disco wer
music styles popular in the 70s. Mixes of these style
paved the way to the transition of new styles like Hi
Hop.

13. Many genres became popular in the 70s, but Disco is the definition of this decade. In the 70s, it was mostly about danceable and rock music.

14. As the 70s saw the rise of iconic artists, like Michael Jackson from Jackson 5, it also saw the setting of an era.

15. The year 1970 marked the end of an era. The Beatles dissolved, suffering internal conflicts. Each went their separate ways appearing on solo albums. Arguably the world's most famous group of all time was no more. The pop and rock music world, which The Beatles had forever changed, would never be the same.

16. Bob Dylan stopped performing in the year 1966 when he had a motorcycle accident. When he reappeared during the 1970s, his voice even got better and made his life worth living again through his poetry and music.

17. The song God Save the Queen was by the band Sex Pistols. The band was formed in 1975 and was responsible for the punk rock movement in the UK.

18. Aerosmith was one of the most popular rock bands in 1976. Steven Tyler became iconic as he was drawn to close comparisons with Mick Jagger.

19. Disco also heavily influenced the fashion of the 70 Although Disco was short-lived, the 70s continuously remembered as the decade of Disc music hits.

20. The 70s and early 80s were the golden ages for Vin Records. At that time, Vinyl Records were affordabl and almost everyone had their own record player Cassette tapes were used too but weren't as popul. as Vinyl Records.

21. Some of the best rock n roll of all time was recorde in the 70s. From David Bowie to Led Zeppelin to Pir Floyd.

22. Enormous music festivals like Woodstock disappeared as quickly as they arrived, due to the inherent danger of attending. Riots, drugs, and violent crowds caused many potentially legendary festivals to be cancelled.

23. Diana Ross left the Supremes for solo fame in 1970.

24. In 1970, Neil Diamond, hit it big with "Cracklin' Rosie" while Simon and Garfunkel impressed audiences with "Bridge Over Troubled Waters."

25. Johnny Cash won two Grammy awards for his song, "A Boy Named Sue" in 1970.

26. Louis Armstrong recovered from illness to throw a famous birthday bash on his "70th birthday" on July 4, 1970. It wasn't known until the 1980s that his true birthday was on August 4, 1901. When he died in 1971, he was actually only 69 years old.

27. A statue was planned to be erected in Armstrong's birthplace of New Orleans. Incredible jazz-only festivals were staged in Monterey and Newport.

28. Two deaths rocked the music world in 1970. On September 18, mercurial guitarist Jimi Hendrix was found dead in London. Less than a month later, on October 4, Janis Joplin died in Hollywood. The dream of peace and love held so dearly by the hippies of the sixties seemed to be vanishing before their very eyes.

29. In 1971, The British Invasion rebooted, featuring several successful tours by several English artists.

30. The Mamas and the Papas were rejuvenated, making a new album in hopes of a tour in 1971.

31. The Beach Boys turned their music to an older audience, those who had listened to them in the earlier days.

32. After a year of breaking up, all of the former Beatles were successful this year, but none more than George Harrison, with "My Sweet Lord." His epic, 3-vinyl box set titled "All Things Must Pass" is considered by many to be Harrison's ultimate masterpiece.

33. The 1971 Newport Jazz festival was cancelled, again due to violence. The Monterey Jazz festival avoided certain peril itself by directing its music toward an older audience.

34. The year 1971 witnessed the death of one of the greatest musicians in the history of humankind. In New York City, on July 6, Louis Armstrong died. "Satchmo" could reach unheard-of notes, and his originality made people want to learn the trumpet just to imitate him. Fortunately, he left us with a massive catalog of over 1,500 records. His influence on modern music, while not necessarily obvious to many, is certain to be felt for centuries to come.

35. 1972 saw the national emergence of "soul music." At one point, the five top-selling records in the US and 11 of the top 20 albums were by African American artists.

36. American rockers went a decidedly softer direction. Neil Young, Three Dog Night and America all released singles that could be described as easy listening.

37. Not so in Britain. Glam rock was in full force as Ziggy Stardust and T. Rex strutted their stuff on stage. Fireworks and other startling effects brought a return to theatrics as Alice Cooper treated his concerts with all the pomp and circumstance of a Broadway play based in Hell.

38. In 1972, The Rolling Stones also toured the US for the first time since 1969 in support of their iconic Exile on Main Street album.

39. The most popular song of 1972, however, belonged to Don McLean with American Pie. The cryptic 8-minute long song captured the hearts and minds of the entire country for the first two months of the year.

40. Rock and pop ruled "Supreme" in 1973. Soul was huge too, featuring legends like Barry White, Stevie Wonder, and more.

41. Reggae was making a breakthrough in the United States, headlined by the Wailers and Jimmy Cliff. Johnny Nash, an American, came out with "Stir It Up" and "I Can See Clearly Now," the first American to have a popular reggae release.

42. Helen Reddy, an Australian, sold millions of copies of her songs, "I Am a Woman" and "Delta Dawn" both topped the charts.

43. The Newport Jazz Festival in New York City was very successful, with jazz enthusiasts coming from around the world to listen to 10 days of jazz music.

44. In 1974, Elton John's popularity soared in both the United States and the United Kingdom. At a concert in California, 75,000 tickets sold out within hours of becoming available.

45. Also in 1974, Crosby, Stills, Nash & Young got back together again, after each of them had attempted to go off on their own.

46. In that same year, Stevie Wonder's second album "Innervisions" was a massive success and Roberta Flack cashed in on her talents as well.

47. In addition, a 12-hour rock show in Ontario, California, made record profits, grossing over $2 million, showcased the Eagles, radio personality Don Imus, and Seals & Crofts.

48. The music world was saddened by the loss of 75-year-old Duke Ellington, one of the most influential jazz artists of all time, in 1974.

49. Aerosmith was one of the most popular groups in 1976, with lead singer Stephen Tyler drawing comparisons to Mick Jagger in more ways than one.

50. Paul McCartney finished a world tour with his band Wings in 1976. The tour, which had begun in Europe the previous year, ended with a tour of the United States and Canada, and was extremely successful.

51. In 1976, Electrified funk became a new musical genre led by Wild Cherry and their lead singer/guitarist Robert Parissi. Their single "Play That Funky Music" sold over a million copies.

52. The Bee Gees exploded into the music world, selling more records than anyone thought possible. They also were the ushers for the disco era, as it was in full swing in 1978. The soundtrack for the movie Saturday Night Fever sold nearly 30 million copies.

II. Most Popular Musicians

Stevie Wonder

1. Birth name: Stevland Hardaway Morris.

2. Born May 13, 1950.

3. Genres: Soul, pop R&B, funk, jazz.

4. He is an American singer, songwriter, musician and record producer.

5. A prominent figure in popular music during the second half of the 20th century, Wonder is one of the most successful songwriters and musicians.

6. A virtual one-man band, his use of synthesizers ar further electronic musical instruments during th 1970s reshaped the conventions of R&B.

7. In 1970, Stevie Wonder turned 20 years old. Havir been a professional recording artist signed to Motow since 1961, Stevie was already a veteran of th industry.

8. During the 1970s, Stevie released a total of eigl studio albums with five tracks reaching number 1 ar many others making it into the US Top 40.

9. Number 1 singles during the 1970s includ Superstition, You Are the Sunshine of My Life, Yc Haven't Done Nothing, I Wish, and Sir Duke.

10. Between 1970 and 1979, Stevie Wonder took home total of 12 Grammy Awards, more than half of the 2 he has received during the course of his career.

Led Zeppelin

1. Led Zeppelin were an English rock band formed in London in 1968.

2. Years active: 1968 – 1980.

3. Genres: Hard rock, blues rock, folk rock, heavy metal.

4. The group consisted of vocalist Robert Plant, guitarist Jimmy Page, bassist/keyboardist John Paul Jones, and drummer John Bonham.

5. With a heavy, guitar-driven sound, they are cited as one of the progenitors of hard rock and heavy metal, although their style drew from a variety of influences, including blues and folk music.

6. Led Zeppelin have been credited as significant impacting the nature of the music industr particularly in the development of album-oriente rock (AOR) and stadium rock.

7. The band broke up due to the passing of drumme John Bonham in October 1980. The cause of deat was asphyxiation from vomit after a heavy night (drinking the night before.

8. The band released a total of eight studio albums, s of which were released during the 1970s.

9. From 1970 to 1979 Led Zeppelin was nominated for Grammy Awards but never won.

10. Between 1999 and 2014, the band did, however, tak home a total of 5 Grammys, 4 of which were Gramm Hall of Fame awards and the 5th for Best Rock Albu in 2014.

Elton John

1. Birth name: Reginald Kenneth Dwight.

2. Born March 25, 1947.

3. Genres: Rock, pop rock, glam rock, soft rock, rhythm and blues.

4. He is an English singer, songwriter, pianist, and composer.

5. Collaborating with lyricist Bernie Taupin since 1967 on more than 30 albums, John has sold over 300 million records, making him one of the best-selling music artists of all time.

6. He has more than fifty Top 40 hits in the UK Single Chart and US Billboard Hot 100, including seve number ones in the UK and nine in the US, as well seven consecutive number-one albums in the US.

7. During the 1970s, Elton John released a total of 1 studio albums (this excludes compilation soundtracks, etc.), six of which made it to number 1 the Billboard 200 Album chart. Six singles made it number 1 in the US Top 40 between 1970 and 1979.

8. During the 1970s, Elton John was nominated for total of 9 Grammy Awards but sadly never won durir this period.

9. In 1994, he was inducted into the Rock and Roll Hall Fame and in 1998 became Sir Elton John after beir knighted by Queen Elizabeth II.

Pink Floyd

1. Pink Floyd were an English rock band formed in London in 1965.

2. Years active: 1965 – 1995, 2005, 2012 – 2014.

3. Genres: Progressive, rock, art rock, psychedelic rock.

4. Gaining an early following as one of the first British psychedelic groups, they were distinguished for their extended compositions, sonic experimentation, philosophical lyrics and elaborate live shows, and became a leading band of the progressive rock genre, cited by some as the greatest progressive rock band of all time.

5. Pink Floyd were founded by Syd Barrett (guitar, lea vocals), Nick Mason (drums), Roger Waters (ba guitar, vocals), Richard Wright (keyboards, vocals) ar Bob Klose (guitars).

6. Between 1970 and 1979, Pink Floyd released a total 9 studio albums including their acclaimed The Da Side of the Moon which sold 15 million units in th United States alone and made it to number 1 in th US Billboard 200 album charts.

7. In total, 3 albums went to number 1 on the L Billboard 200 during this time.

8. Just one song, Another Brick in the Wall (Part II) mac it to number 1 in the US Top 40 during the 1970s.

9. The band was inducted into the Rock and Roll Hall Fame in 1996.

The Rolling Stones

1. The Rolling Stones are an English rock band formed in London in 1962.

2. Years active: 1962 – present.

3. Genres: Rock, blues, rock and roll.

4. Diverging from the pop rock of the early-1960s, the Rolling Stones pioneered the gritty, heavier-driven sound that came to define hard rock.

5. Their first stable line-up was vocalist Mick Jagger, multi-instrumentalist Brian Jones, guitarist Keith Richards, drummer Charlie Watts, and bassist Bill Wyman.

6. During the 1970s, The Rolling Stones released 6 stud
   albums two of which went to number 1 on the U
   Billboard 200 album chart.

7. Between 1970 and 1979, the band had 3 tracks th
   made it to number 1 in the US Top 40.

8. They were nominated for just a single Grammy Awai
   during the 70s but, unfortunately, did not win.

9. The Rolling Stones were inducted into the Rock ar
   Roll Hall of Fame in 1989.

Eagles

1. The Eagles are an American rock band formed in Los Angeles in 1971.

2. Years active: 1971–1980, 1994–2016, 2017–present.

3. Genres: Rock, country, rock, soft rock, folk rock.

4. Founding members Glenn Frey (guitars, vocals), Don Henley (drums, vocals), Bernie Leadon (guitars, vocals) and Randy Meisner (bass guitar, vocals) were recruited by Linda Ronstadt as band members, some touring with her, and all playing on her third solo album, before venturing out on their own on David Geffen's new Asylum Records label.

5. The band released a total of 7 studio albums, 6 of which were released during the 1970s.

6. Three of their 1970s albums made it to number 1 the US Billboard 200 album charts.

7. Five tracks released during the 70s went to number in the US Top 40.

8. During the 1970s, The Eagles won four of their s Grammy Nominations.

9. The band was inducted into the Rock and Roll Hall of Fame in 1998.

Marvin Gaye

1. Birth name: Marvin Pentz Gay Jr.

2. April 2, 1939 – April 1, 1984.

3. Genres: R&B, soul, psychedelic soul, funk, jazz, pop.

4. He was an American singer, songwriter, and record producer.

5. He helped to shape the sound of Motown in the 1960s, first as an in-house session player and later as a solo artist with a string of hits, earning him the nicknames "Prince of Motown" and "Prince of Soul".

6. By 1970, at the age of 31, Gaye already had 9 years experience in the music industry.

7. Between 1970 and 1979, Marvin Gaye released a total of six studio albums including the famous Let's Get On which made it to number 2 on the US Billboard 200 album charts.

8. During the same time, two singles made it to number 1 on the US Top 40.

9. Marvin Gaye was nominated for six Grammy awards during the 1970s but unfortunately didn't manage to win.

10. He was inducted into the Rock and Roll Hall of Fame in 1987.

Queen

1. Queen are a British rock band formed in London in 1970.

2. Years active: 1970 – present.

3. Genre: Rock.

4. Their classic line-up was Freddie Mercury (lead vocals, piano), Brian May (guitar, vocals), Roger Taylor (drums, vocals) and John Deacon (bass).

5. Their earliest works were influenced by progressive rock, hard rock and heavy metal, but the band gradually ventured into more conventional and radio-

friendly works by incorporating further styles, such a
arena rock and pop rock.

6. Between 1970 and 1979, Queen released a total c
    seven studio albums.

7. Two albums made it to number 1 in the UK's Offici
    Album Charts but never got higher than number 3 c
    the US Billboard 200 album charts.

8. Queen managed just a single US Top 40 number
    with Crazy Little Thing Called Love in 1979.

9. The band was nominated for two Grammy Awarc
    during the 70s but failed to win.

10. Queen was inducted into the Rock and Roll Hall c
    Fame in 2001.

James Brown

1. Full name: James Joseph Brown.

2. May 3, 1933 – December 25, 2006.

3. Genres: Funk, soul, rhythm and blues.

4. He was an American singer, songwriter, dancer, musician, record producer, and bandleader.

5. The central progenitor of funk music and a major figure of 20th-century music, he is often referred to by the honorific nicknames "Godfather of Soul", "Mr. Dynamite", and "Soul Brother No. 1".

6. In a career that lasted over 50 years, he influence the development of several music genres.

7. Between 1970 and 1979, Brown released 23 of his studio albums.

8. Sadly, none of his 1970s album releases made it number 1 in the US Billboard 200 album chart however, Brown did get a number 1 in the Billboar R&B album charts with The Payback released in 1973

9. While many of his singles made it into the US Top 4 James Brown never made it to number 1 during th 1970s.

10. James Brown was one of the first inductees to th Rock and Roll Hall of Fame in 1986.

The Who

1. The Who are an English rock band formed in London in 1964.

2. Years active: 1964–1983, 1989, 1996–1997, 1999–present.

3. Genres: Rock, hard rock, pop.

4. Their classic lineup consisted of lead singer Roger Daltrey, guitarist and singer Pete Townshend, bass guitarist and singer John Entwistle, and drummer Keith Moon.

5. They are considered one of the most influential rock bands of the 20th century and have sold over 100 million records worldwide.

6. The band released just four albums during the 1970s
    with two making it to number 2 in US Billboard 200
    album charts.

7. While many of The Who's singles made it into the U
    Top 40, none made it to the number 1 position durin
    the 1970s.

8. The band wasn't nominated for any Grammy Award
    during the 70s but were inducted into the Rock an
    Roll Hall of Fame in 1990.

III. Most Popular Movies

1. "Death Wish" (1974) was directed by Michael Winner and written by Brian Garfield (novel) and Wendell Mayes (screenplay). Four sequels were made following this movie: "Death Wish II" (1982), "Death Wish 3" (1985), "Death Wish 4: The Crackdown" (1987) and "Death Wish V: The Face of Death" (1994).

2. "Dog Day Afternoon" (1975) was directed by Sidney Lumet and written by Frank Pierson and P.F. Kluge. It won one Oscar and was nominated for a further five. It is based on a true story that occurred in the early seventies, the real bank robber was called John Wojtowicz.

3. "Airport" '77 (1977) was directed by Jerry Jamesc and written by Arthur Hailey, Michael Scheff, Dav Spector, H.A.L. Craig and Charles Kuenstle. It wa nominated for two Oscars. To prepare for his role Ja Lemmon went to flight training school.

4. "Kramer vs. Kramer" was directed by Robert Bentc and written by Avery Corman and Robert Benton. won five Oscars and four Golden Globes. At the tim of filming Dustin Hoffman was going through a mess divorce himself and often used the emotions he wa feeling to enhance his acting.

5. "Halloween" (1978) was directed by John Carpente and he co-wrote it with Debra Hill. It was made with very low budget but went on to make over 45 millic at the US box office. "Halloween" was Jamie Le Curtis' first movie role.

6. "Silver Streak" (1976) was written by Colin Higgins an directed by Arthur Hiller. It was nominated for on Oscar and one Golden Globe. It was the first of fou films that starred Richard Pryor and Gene Wilde together.

7. The original "Airport" was released in 1970. Th movie was based on a 1968 book and centere around an airport manager's problems with snowstorm and a suicide bomber on a plane. Bu Lancaster played the airport manager.

Four years later "Airport 1975" was released. The film focused on a mid-air collision and the efforts of the surviving crew to bring the plane to a safe landing.

8. "Saturday Night Fever" is among the most famous dance films of all time. The story of a nobody becoming a somebody in a dance club is very inspirational and, as a result, people have found this to be an entertaining film. For the filming of the movie John Travolta ran two miles a day and danced for three hours to get in shape. In the end, Travolta dropped 20 pounds.

9. "Alien", was one of Sigourney Weaver's most highly regarded movies. It was a psychological/science-fiction/thriller that featured a predatory Alien killing off the crew members of a spaceship. The movie never failed to exhilarate, and therefore, the viewer knew that the director accomplished his work.

10. "Last Tango in Paris" (1972) was directed by Bernard Bertolucci and he co-wrote it with Franco Arcalli. was nominated for two Oscars and two Golde Globes. Because of the film's sexual content, it wa banned in both Chile and Italy.

11. "Papillon" (1973) was directed by Franklin J. Schaffne and written by Henri Charrière (book) and Dalto Trumbo and Lorenzo Semple Jr (screenplay). It wa nominated for one Oscar and one Golden Globe. Th film is based loosely on a true story and the mai character of Henri is nicknamed 'Papillon ' because (his butterfly tattoo. The real life Papillon, Hen Charrière, died just a few months before the film wa released.

12. "The Texas Chain Saw Massacre" (1974) was directe by Tobe Hooper and written by Kim Henkel and Tob Hooper. The actor who played the 113-year-ol grandfather of the cannibalistic family was only 20 i the time of filming. In 1990 the film was inducted int the Horror Hall of Fame.

13. "10 Rillington Place" (1971) is based on macabre tru events in London during the 1940s and 1950s. Richar Attenborough plays evil serial killer John Christie while John Hurt plays Timothy Evans, the fall guy wh was hanged for two of the murders.

14. "The Goodbye Girl" (1977) was directed by Herbert Ross and written by Neil Simon. It won one Oscar and four Golden Globes. The film's theme song "Goodbye Girl" (1977) was written and recorded by David Gates and it went to number fifteen in the US.

15. "The Amityville Horror" (1979) was written by Sandor Stern and Jay Anson and directed by Stuart Rosenberg. It was nominated for one Oscar and one Golden Globe. There have been several sequels, remakes and spin offs since (some official, some not) such as "Amityville II: The Possession" (1982) and "The Amityville Curse" (1990).

IV. Most Popular Actors

Jack Nicholson

1. Birth name: John Joseph Nicholson.

2. Born April 22, 1937.

3. He is an American actor and filmmaker whose career has spanned more than 60 years.

4. He is known for having played a wide range of starring and supporting roles, including comic characters, romantic leads, anti-heroes and villains. In many of his films, he played the "eternal outsider, the sardonic drifter", someone who rebels against the social structure.

5. His twelve Academy Award nominations make him the most nominated male actor in the Academy's history.

6. He has won the Academy Award for Best Actor twice, once for One Flew Over the Cuckoo's Nest (1975) and once for As Good as It Gets (1997).

7. He is one of only three male actors to win three Academy Awards, and one of only two actors to be nominated for an Academy Award for acting in every decade from the 1960s to the 2000s.

8. In 1994, he became one of the youngest actors to be awarded the American Film Institute's Life Achievement Award.

9. Nicholson is a collector of 20th-century and contemporary art, including the work of Henri Matisse, Tamara de Lempicka, Andy Warhol and Jack Vettriano.

10. Nicholson is a fan of the New York Yankees and Los Angeles Lakers.

Diane Keaton

1. Full name: Diane Hall Keaton.

2. Born January 5, 1946.

3. She is an American actress and filmmaker.

4. Known for her idiosyncratic personality and dressin
   style, she has received an Academy Award, a BAFT
   Award, two Golden Globe Awards, and the AFI Lif
   Achievement Award.

5. Keaton opposes plastic surgery. She told Mor
   magazine in 2004, "I'm stuck in this idea that I need t
   be authentic ... My face needs to look the way I feel."

Marlon Brando

1. Birth name: Marlon Brando Jr.

2. April 3, 1924 – July 1, 2004.

3. He was an American actor and film director with a career spanning 60 years, during which he won many accolades, including two Academy Awards for Best Actor, three BAFTA Awards for Best Foreign Actor and two Golden Globe Awards for Best Actor — Motion Picture Drama.

4. He is regarded as arguably the greatest and mo influential actor in 20th-century film.

5. Brando was also an activist for many causes, notab the civil rights movement and various Nativ American movements.

6. Brando was ranked by the American Film Institute a the fourth-greatest movie star among male mov stars whose screen debuts occurred in or befor 1950.

7. He was one of only six actors named in 1999 by Tim magazine in its list of the 100 Most Important Peop of the Century. In this list, Time also designate Brando as the "Actor of the Century".

Ellen Burstyn

1. Birth name: Edna Rae Gillooly.

2. Born December 7, 1932.

3. She is an American actress.

4. Known for her portrayal of complicated women in dramas, Burstyn is the recipient of numerous accolades, including an Academy Award, two Primetime Emmy Awards, and a Tony Award, one of

the few performers to achieve the "Triple Crown of Acting".

5. During the 1970s, Burstyn was active in the movement to free convicted boxer Rubin "Hurricane" Carter from jail.

6. Since 2000, she has been co-president of the Actors Studio, alongside Al Pacino and Alec Baldwin.

7. In 2013, she was inducted into the American Theatre Hall of Fame for her work on stage.

Robert Redford

1. Full name: Charles Robert Redford Jr.

2. Born August 18, 1936.

3. He is an American actor, director, and activist.

4. He is the recipient of various accolades, including two Academy Awards, a British Academy Film Award, three Golden Globe Awards, the Cecil B. DeMille Award, and the Presidential Medal of Freedom.

5. Appearing on stage in the late 1950s, Redford television career began in 1960, including a appearance on The Twilight Zone in 1962.

6. In 2014, Time magazine named him one of the 10 most influential people in the world.

Faye Dunaway

1. Full name: Dorothy Faye Dunaway.

2. Born January 14, 1941.

3. She is an American actress.

4. She is the recipient of many accolades, including a Academy Award, an Emmy Award (Primetime), thre Golden Globe Awards, and a BAFTA Award.

5. In 2011, the government of France made her an Officer of the Order of Arts and Letters.

6. Dunaway is a devout Catholic and has said that she attends morning mass regularly. She converted in the late 1990s and, until then, was a lifelong Protestant.

Gene Hackman

1. Full name: Eugene Allen Hackman.

2. Born January 30, 1930.

3. He is an American retired actor, novelist, and United States Marine.

4. In a career that has spanned more than six decade
    Hackman has won two Academy Awards, four Golde
    Globes, one Screen Actors Guild Award, and tw
    BAFTAs.

5. Hackman is a supporter of the Democratic Party, an
    was proud to be included on Nixon's Enemies Lis
    However, he has spoken fondly of Republica
    president Ronald Reagan.

6. He is an avid fan of the Jacksonville Jaguars an
    regularly attended Jaguars games as a guest of th
    head coach Jack Del Rio. Their friendship goes back t
    Del Rio's playing days at the University of Souther
    California.

Meryl Streep

1. Birth name: Mary Louise Streep.

2. Born June 22, 1949.

3. She is an American actress and singer.

4. Often described as the "best actress of her generation", Streep is particularly known for her versatility and accents.

5. Her accolades include a record 21 Academy Award nominations, winning three, and a record 32 Golden Globe Award nominations, winning nine.

6.   She was awarded the AFI Life Achievement Award
     2004, Gala Tribute from the Film Society of Linco
     Center in 2008, and Kennedy Center Honor in 201
     for her contribution to American culture, throug
     performing arts.

7.   President Barack Obama awarded her the 201
     National Medal of Arts, and in 2014, the Presidenti
     Medal of Freedom.

8.   In 2003, the government of France made her
     Commander of the Order of Arts and Letters.

Al Pacino

1. Full name: Alfredo James Pacino.

2. Born April 25, 1940.

3. He is an American actor and filmmaker. In a career spanning over five decades, he has received many awards and nominations, including an Academy Award, two Tony Awards, and two Primetime Emmy Awards.

4. He is one of the few performers to have received the Triple Crown of Acting.

5. Pacino has three children. The eldest, Julie Mar[...] (born 1989), is his daughter with acting coach Ja[...] Tarrant. He has twins, son Anton James and daught[...] Olivia Rose (born January 25, 2001), with actre[...] Beverly D'Angelo, with whom he had a relationsh[...] from 1996 until 2003. He has never been married.

6. Pacino had a ten-year relationship with Argentin[...] actress Lucila Polak from 2008 to 2018.

Liv Ullmann

1. Full name: Liv Johanne Ullmann.

2. Born December 16, 1938.

3. She is a Norwegian actress and film director.

4. Recognized as one of the greatest European actresses, Ullmann attained global recognition and acclaim with her numerous collaborations with filmmaker Ingmar Bergman.

5. Ullmann is the recipient of numerous accolades, including a British Academy Film Award, a Golden Globe Award, in addition to nominations for two Academy Awards.

6. Ullmann won a Golden Globe Award for Best Actress – Motion Picture Drama in 1972 for the film The Emigrants (1971), and has been nominated for another four.

7. In 2000, she was nominated for the Palme d'Or for her second directorial feature film, Faithless.

8. She has also received two BAFTA Award nominations. She was twice nominated for the Academy Award for Best Actress for the Swedish dramas The Emigrants (1971), and Face to Face (1976), making her the first actor to garner multiple nominations for foreign language films.

V. Fashion

Trends in the 70s

Continuing the 1960s fashion theme of individual styl
flares, platforms, fringing and suede dominated the 70
fashion era with icons aplenty; Joni Mitchell, Cher, Bianc
Jagger and more making huge waves in the style world.

So many trends defined the 70s, not least the boho tren
which Sienna Millar revived in the 00s. Peasant blouses, t
dye, bell sleeves, crochet dresses and bell bottoms were a
staples of that trend.

The short skirt peaked in that decade, with icons such a
Jane Birkin and Twiggie inspiring their followers to wea
shorter hems and taller boots.

ut while the hippie movement was prevalent, it didn't stop
eople from dressing up, judging by the cool crowd at
udio 54. Satin, off-the-shoulder dresses, jumpsuit and
mé gowns were all the rage, as were crop tops and skirts.

970s fashion designers

o many fashion designers defined the 70s fashion era. The
te Karl Lagerfeld worked for another major fashion label –
hloé at the time. His vision defined the house's trademark
oho direction, an aesthetic that current designer Clare
Vaight Keller still nods to today.

What did real women wear in the seventies? Barbar
Hulanicki's London boutique Biba experienced a huge sale
boom, selling bell bottom power suits (cat covered, c
course) and smock dresses in saturated colours, all a
affordable price points. The roots for high street fashio
were firmly planted and, thanks to an unrivalled ma
ordering service, women around the country were able t
experience fast fashion for the first time.

Diane Von Furstenberg made her now-iconic wrap dress i
1974 after setting out to create a relaxed, silk jersey dres
that could suit every woman's body shape with ease
Originally available in a small range of very seventies print
she was quickly given the cover of business bible Newswee
and declared the 'most marketable designer since Coc
Chanel.' The magazine was right, and by 1976 Diane ha
sold over 5 million of the dress worldwide, building a lastin
fashion empire in the process. A true seventies icon.

ne (now legendary) designer Roy Halston Frowick shot to
ame in this decade thanks to his minimalistic draped gowns
nd his greatest invention, the jersey halter dress. You'd find
m at Studio 54 with Elizabeth Taylor on one arm and Liza
linelli on the other.

/omen were hooked on Laura Ashley's romantic
lhouettes and floral-drenched prints when it came to
etting their 1970s fashion fix. When they were first
reated, the Edwardian-style dresses and vintage-look
abrics divided opinion amongst the more fashion-forward.
'hey're not particularly clothes for making a splash in a
ramatic place,' the designer justified at the time. 'They're
mple garments to wear at home, and when you get home
erhaps you need the security of nostalgia.' Personally, we
ove them.

The new queen of punk Vivienne Westwood was about to make fashion history when she opened her boutique Too Fast To Live, Too Young To Die on Kings Road in 1971. Two years later, she changed the shop's name to SEX, turning fetishes into fashion under the catchy tagline 'rubberwear for the office.' It was innovative, expressive, and the people loved it – it's no wonder she ended up becoming one of fashion's biggest names.

Who influenced 1970s fashion?

There were many poster girls for 70s fashion, but Joni Mitchell was undoubtedly one of the seventies' ultimate style icons – and with good reason. She wore tie dye blouses, earth-goddess hair and billowing kaftans like no ther, usually completing her trademark look with bare feet nd a guitar in hand.

her released a whopping 10 albums in the 70s meaning, uite simply, that she was absolutely everywhere. From ore-is-more prints to epic perms, she tried every trend the ecade had to offer with gusto, meaning she was seventies shion personified.

The late David Bowie's alter ego skewed ideas about gende and fashion in the seventies; the star would perform i spray on leotards, foil flares and a whole lotta face pain The ultimate style chameleon, Bowie transformed his loo again and again throughout his career, but this will alway be the moment where he changed 1970s fashion an beyond forever.

Post The Supremes, Diana Ross was all about lila eyeshadow, loose wrap dresses and XXL hoop earrings. Lik Cher, she whipped up an incredible nine albums in her firs decade as a solo artist and was a key style icon, too. We'r sure the sepia tones and retro wardrobe choices in thi picture must have inspired American Hustle?

lton John, Debbie Harry, Farrah Fawcett and pretty much ny celebrity frequenting Studio 54 could be trusted to wow eople with their outfits.

VI. Trivia Answer Keys

1.	A	18.	C
2.	A	19.	B
3.	C	20.	D
4.	A	21.	D
5.	B	22.	B
6.	D	23.	B
7.	A	24.	C
8.	B	25.	B
9.	D	26.	D
10.	B	27.	C
11.	B	28.	C
12.	C	29.	A
13.	D	30.	B
14.	B	31.	B
15.	D	32.	D
16.	B	33.	A
17.	A	34.	B

35.	B	53.	C
36.	C	54.	B
37.	A	55.	C
38.	D	56.	D
39.	D	57.	C
40.	D	58.	A
41.	D	59.	D
42.	A	60.	A
43.	C	61.	D
44.	D	62.	B
45.	C	63.	D
46.	D	64.	B
47.	B	65.	A
48.	A	66.	C
49.	B	67.	C
50.	D	68.	B
51.	B	69.	A
52.	A	70.	C

Is there anything you would like to add?

Your best memories with the 1970's Art Acts:

Stick your memorable photo about the 1970's here

THANK YOU FOR ENJOYING THIS TRIVIA!

Printed in Great Britain
by Amazon

13488638R00059